would like t
me hunt on

Authored by

Randy Jewett

Copywrite to Randy Jewett

February 1 2018

THE DIARY OF A HUNTER

BY RANDY A JEWETT

Diary of a Hunter

Spring Turkey Season

April 1st - 2016

Started my scouting today for turkeys and came up empty morning and night. This means turkey hunting is thirty days away.

April 2nd – 2016

Got up this morning and checked some of my old hot spots in Montgomery and didn't find any birds. Went to Berkshire in the afternoon and found just as many as I did this morning.

April 3rd - 2016

Got up and checked Montgomery again and didn't see anything again. I went back in the evening and couldn't find any birds. I had seen birds around all winter so where are they now?

April 4th –2016

I didn't go scouting this morning and don't intend to go tonight. I have about ten places that I check for birds and so far these places are not producing. I have two blinds that I set-up. One spot will get one automatically and I choose the second spot according to what I see, how often, how many, and the size of the birds.

April 5th – 2016

I went back to Montgomery and didn't see a thing. I stayed at home that afternoon and the next week or so. One night it came to me to go to Black Falls. This place has been good to me in the past and I haven't checked it out this year.

April 26th – 2016

I went to my spot on the Black Falls Road and sat beside the road waiting for the sun to come up. The sun had been up for twenty minutes when I saw the turkeys coming my way. One was a big tom and he had eight hens. They were in the pasture but stayed close to the woods. They were going behind the barn so I lost track of them for a while. I got out of the truck and went over to the barn and they were feeding on the manure pile. I didn't want to spook them so I left.

I got back there in the evening and parked in the same place. It looked as if I wasn't going to see them When I happened to glance into my mirror and they were crossing the road behind me. They went into the pasture and headed down the trail they were on this morning.

April 27th – 2016

I was back at the spot again and the birds came up through just like clockwork. That's the way it's supposed to be. I went to Lee's door and we had a nice long talk. It seems that the turkeys go into the barn and eat the cows grain right in front of them. When the cows would try to eat, the turkeys would peck them. He said to shoot everyone I could but to be very careful of the cows. He said the turkeys should weigh up pretty good because they are grain fed. I went back that evening and saw them again.

April 28th – 2016

I went back up there and didn't see the birds in the morning. After a while I went down the road and turned around and went back up to Lee's and drove by his house. I looked back behind the barn and there were the birds. That evening I brought my friend with me and he said that the tom was a good one.

April 29th – 2016

I didn't get there until noon so I could set up my blind. After careful consideration I picked the spot that I thought would be best to get that tom. I went back later and watched them walk right by the blind. Just can't wait until Sunday morning.

April 30th – 2016

I couldn't go check on the birds because of my PD fundraiser.

May 1st – 2016

This is the opening day of the 2016 turkey season. My friend and I were there at 4:10 am. I don't usually use a light to get to my blinds but he had one on his hat and I

wasn't quite in the right spot. We got in the blind and got our seats set where we wanted them. We relaxed until 4:45 when the tom started gobbling. He was close so I started looking out the back window and there he was. The tom was on a small limb and in full strut a beautiful sight. I looked around and his hens were in another tree. I
had decided not to set out decoys or to call. I figured they always come right there any way so why take a chance of them getting scared of a decoy. We had ranged the area and picked out bushes, limbs and other things at 20 yards. Well it

had been light out for some time when I hear them leave their roost. The hens came first and landed inside our twenty yard markers. Then he came in right next to a bush we had for 20 yards but I needed him to take a couple of steps to have a clear shot. He did just what he was supposed to do and when I squeezed the trigger it was all done. We brought him to the store to get it weighed and measured. It was a nice bird at 20 pounds with an eight and one half inch beard and 7/8 inch spurs. Thank you lord. Now we start scouting again. I didn't find any birds Sunday evening.

May 2nd – 2016

The second day and I'm going to my blind on Marshall's and saw nothing.

I went looking for birds in the afternoon and didn't see any.

May 3rd - 2016

I went back to the blind I shot my tom from but this time I put a hen decoy out. A hen came in and said good morning to the decoy and left. I left right behind her and started scouting again and saw nothing.

May 4th - 2016

I couldn't go hunting because of a doctors'

appointment. But I took a ride in the afternoon and spotted a huge tom with a hen just past Frank's barn on the lower side of the road.

May 5th – 2016

I decided not to set up my decoys and to sit so I could lean against a tree and watch the pasture. It was getting light out when I heard what sounded like something walking in the leaves behind me. I tried turning my head to see what it was but I didn't see anything. I was getting relaxed again and the leaves started rustling. I looked around but couldn't see anything. Then it happened again and I looked up in the tree and there was a turkey up there taking a crap. I got to looking around and the tree next to me had a turkey in it. I knew two turkeys were here last night and I can see two turkeys so all I have to do is to determine which is which. They were still in the tree well after daylight when I heard one gobble. It didn't come from the tree that I was against so I figured it was the other bird. I pulled my gun up and fired a shot. The turkey fell out of the tree but as soon as it hit the ground it was flying back into the tree. I thought he was hit hard because my nose was hit hard but I wasn't bleeding so it's okay. I checked my tree to see if the turkey was still there but it was gone. I look back at my bird and he was still there. I took my binoculars out and started checking that bird out. Boy was he small and I couldn't see a beard. There were some other hunters a couple hundred yards from me so I shot it again. He came out of the tree and ran into a brush pile. So I slowly approached the brush pile that is after I stopped bleeding. He must have seen me because he ran out of the brush pile and into the brook. On the edge of the brook was a hole and he had his head stuck in the hole so he thought he was safe. I grabbed the bird and finished him off. It turned out to be a hen with a 4.5 inch beard that weighed 10 pounds. Time to start scouting again to help Brian get a turkey. It didn't take too long to locate a nice tom.

May 6th – 2016

Friday Brian wasn't feeling well so we have to wait another day. I went up there and saw the bird come out and catch up with some hens. That evening I put him to bed but it was in a different place.

May 7th – 2016

I got there about 3:30 to try to find the perfect spot to

ambush a turkey. Brian got there about 4:00 and together we picked out a spot and put out one hen decoy. We got in our spots and it had been light for a while when Brian said let's get this show on the road. I did 5 yelps on my box call and didn't get an answer. We looked over in the pasture and a tom was running straight at us. Brian said maybe we shouldn't call any more so I stopped. The tom went right to the decoy and I kept wondering why he wasn't shooting. The

 Bird went right by him and into the ditch and was going away when I let out a yelp.

The bird spun around and headed right to Brian. Brian needed to turn just a tad but couldn't with the tom looking right at him. The tom stopped and picked it's head up to look at the decoy and the old Mossberg went off and Brian had turkey number one. It weighed eighteen pounds with a nine inch beard. Congrats to Brian who always says it's better to be lucky than good. We are now back to scouting again.

May 8th – 2016

Didn't find any birds today.

May 9th - 2016

I went back to where Brian got his bird and saw

two big toms strutting in the meadow about 25 yards away. I went and got him to show him the birds but when we got back they were about two hundred yards away. That night we put them to bed.

May 10th - 12th - 2016

I have checked on the toms this week and have seen them every morning and night. They may be coming out or going in the woods a little different each time but they are always there. Brian doesn't work on Friday so that will be the big day. We put the birds to bed Thursday night.

May 13th - 2016

Here we are Friday morning about 4:00 am and we are set up with two hen decoys. It's now past shooting time and we haven't seen or heard a turkey so I try a few yelps and wait, no response. I try a different call and no response. I have Brian call and no response. About fifteen minutes later we spot a hen heading away from us at 300 yards. We wait another fifteen minutes and decide to see where the hen went. We went past the house and the barn then toward the woods. There is a high spot in the pasture and you have to be almost to the top in order to see over it and to the woods. As we approached the high spot we ran into the two toms. They were strutting for the hen. I don't think that they saw us but as soon as I called they started running away. When Brian called they stopped and gobbled. We played with them for what seemed like hours but it was probably a few minutes. They were working towards the woods all the time, finally they went into the woods and they would gobble just inside so Brian made a mad dash to the edge of the woods but couldn't see them. After a while we couldn't hear them anymore. We decided to go to the next road over and try some calling maybe they will be over there. We tried and we struck out again. We couldn't hunt the other place anymore because the owners were coming back home. We had an agreement that as long as they are away we can hunt but when they are home we stay away. We are scouting again.

May 14th – 2016

I didn't see any birds morning or evening.

May 15th – 2016

I put three birds to bed but I couldn't tell what they were.

May 16th – 2016

I waited for the birds to come out but didn't see them so I took a little ride. I came back through around 6:30 and the birds were out I was pretty sure one was a tom. In the evening I put them to bed.

May 17th – 2016

I got up early and grabbed my bucket and went up to the back meadow where I have been seeing the turkeys. I sat there for a couple of hours then about 6:10 I saw them coming. The first two looked like hens but the third one never let me see him. I told Brian about the birds and we put them to bed tonight. He couldn't go until Saturday because he was working.

May 21st – 2016

Brian went by himself this morning knowing that these birds come out late. I talked to him later and he didn't have a bird. I asked him what happened? He tells me that he was there at 4:20 and finds a spot to sit. He doesn't see or hear anything so he leaves at 5:20 and goes for a short ride. He comes back to the field and the birds are out there. He tries to sneak up on them but gets busted and they ran away. I asked him what time did you come back through and see the turkeys? 6:15 was his answer. I rest my case. I didn't locate any more birds and called it a season.

Bear Season 2016

August 17th – 2016

I went to Burn's today to check out the corn and the sandbar and to put up my blind. The corn didn't look as if it would be ready in two weeks. So I check the sand bar and its covered with bushes 2-3 foot high. There are some bamboo growing too. This is going to make good cover for a bear which means that I have to be on the ball. I put my blind in the usual place and got the first batch of bamboo cut down.

August 24th – 2016

Went back to the corn field to check the corn and it is ready for the bear to eat. I went to the sand bar and found three sets of tracks. One was a cub or small bear, one was probably a 100 pounder, and the other one we called pie plate because his feet were huge and he probably was too. I cleaned and cut some more bamboo by my blind. The season starts Thursday the first of September and I can't wait.

September 1st – 2016

I don't usually hunt in the morning but because of the sign and the number of men with hounds around I thought I would try it. I got in my blind at 5:10 and at 6:10 I saw my first bear. And as many of you know I am not a trophy hunter so look out bear. He came out and stayed in the brush and never gave me a shot. I sat until 9:00 and left.

I got back at 2:00 in the afternoon and left at 8:10. It would have made for a long sit except for seeing two buck. One had a nice rack and the other looked like a spike but they were more than a foot long and came up and curled around like he had a rack.

September 2nd – 2016

Got in the blind about 5:00 and at 5:50 a bear came out and gave me a broadside shot at 75 yards. He appeared to have dropped in his tracks. I waited 10 minutes and I hadn't seen it move a muscle so I went to get my bear. When I got there the bear was gone. I looked for him, blood, or tracks. I did find a spot that looked like he was dragging himself into the bamboo. I went to get help and after a quite some time I got 4 people and one dog. The dog picked the scent up right off and he was headed for the mountains.

I tried following but slipped trying to cross the brook. My Insulated boots had a liner and they soaked up the water and my boots filled up. I ended up laying on my back in the brook. I was wearing a backpack with dry clothes and that was filling with water. I was in a fine mess. My rifle was under water all this time. I finally got rolled over and on my hands and knees and crawled to shore. I took my boots off and poured the water out then pulled the liner out and wrung it out. I took off my heavy winter coat. I was wringing everything from my back pack when they got a call from the guy with the dog. He told us that the bear was right in front of him. He hadn't seen it but heard it. He wanted me up there in a hurry. This meant I had to get my crap together. I got everything back on and went to find the guy with the dog. I caught up to his partner first. He grabbed my gun and told me to get rid of the backpack and the heavy coat. I still couldn't keep up with him. Then I see them coming back and they said that they had gotten into a lot of bear sign. They also found pie plates track. My bear had gotten into a bunch of ledges so they had to quit. I offered to pay them but they said no it's what we like to do.

I got to the blind about 4:30 that afternoon and didn't see anything until 5:30. I looked down to the river and saw a fawn run downstream and a little later it came back up the river. Then five minutes later it comes right at me on the sand bar and turns where the bear went through and there was a coyote three feet behind it. I didn't have time to shoot so I say to the fawn to come back around and I would take care of its problem. I didn't see it again. It was 6:30 when I look out of my left hand window and see a coyote coming right at me. I pulled my gun to my shoulder and pointed it out the front window and when it walked in front of me I squeezed the trigger. The coyote took off biting at his shoulder. I got out and went down to find my coyote. I found a lot of blood and he hadn't gone very far maybe 75 yards. I also saw a fresh bear track. I went back to the blind and sat until dark.

September 3rd – 2016
I got there around 5:10 I

stayed there until 8:00 then I went down to the beach and didn't find anything. I went home and didn't go out tonight because I was going out for supper.

I was told that the guys with the bear hounds took a man out bear hunting and he shot a 280 pound bear. This was the man who approached me at the Springfield Mass Sportsman Show. My friend and I were selling bear hunts in New Brunswick. He wanted to hunt with hounds in VT. He gave me his number and when I got home I gave his number to two people with hounds. The guy that tried helping me was one of them. I think that this was his fourth year. The guy gave me a call but I was hunting. I tried calling back but didn't get in touch with him.

September 4th – 2016

I got to the blind around the same time. I sat for two hours then went and checked for tracks. I didn't find anything fresh and was going to leave until I heard voices in the corn. I got back in my blind and then the dogs opened up. It sounded like they went toward the covered bridge. The dogs were out of my hearing in a few minutes. I sat there for another hour hoping they would come back, no such luck. On the way out I see a truck coming at me in the meadow. The truck had a dog box on it. It was the bear man and he asked me if I would like to shoot a bear. Well dah I said yes and he lets his hounds out. I told him somebody just chased a bear out of the corn, he went in any way and came back in twenty minutes empty handed except for the hounds. I thought they would suggest another place. They said we'll see you later and maybe try this spot if you're not here some morning. I told him that it would be better if I was here then I could shoot a bear if it came by me or treed. They said good luck and left.

September 5th – 2016

Didn't get to the blind until 5:50 and sat until 7:30. I didn't see anything so I checked for tracks and found none so I left. When I got to the Dutchburn farm there were people all over. Some had cameras, some had guns and some had dogs. I went by and turned around by the covered bridge and went back by. This time they had a bear going so I went up by the Archambeault farm and got out to listen for the dogs. They sounded like they were coming right at me. All of a sudden they turned and went toward the back pasture so I drove part way up the hill and got out and the dogs were right there in front of me. I turned him again. Now he was going back to the corn so I went to the back pasture but he came back and was heading toward the road. I went as fast as I could to get to the road and the dogs were right beside my truck. The bear was going toward Stan's place when I heard a semi automatic rifle fire five shots and shortly after the dogs stopped barking. When I went back down a couple of rigs were turning around in the road and then they were gone. I went home.

I didn't go back in the evening.

September 6th – 2016

Got to the blind at 5:30 and sat until 7:40. I checked for tracks but couldn't find any so I head for home. As I was walking to my truck I thought of another place to check, the big corn piece by the new road.

It was 10:50 and I was walking along the river bank looking for tracks finding a few nice ones. As I approached the ditch I walked slow and as quietly as I could and I peeked around the corner and didn't see anything in the ditch then I heard something and look up and on this big blowdown is a big bear. I see him jump down to another limb and then into the weeds that were four foot tall and he was gone. I informed Brian about what I saw but he didn't act interested. I went back to my blind this afternoon and saw nothing again.

September 7th – 2016

I got to the blind at 5:30 and sat until 11:00. I went down and checked for tracks and didn't see any sign of anything crossing there. I went to my blind and grabbed a few things and went to the truck. On my way home I stopped at Blair's sugarhouse and got permission to hunt there for deer hunting. That afternoon I went to the big corn piece on Doug's land. I hunted on the end of the ditch near the spot that I had seen the bear. I brought a slingshot that I had made and shot some stones into the big patch of bamboo that I was next to. It wasn't long before there was at least one bear walking back and forth grunting, growling and clicking his teeth but he never let me see him. I thought I could hear someone calling my name so I left to check it out. When I got to the meadow I didn't see anyone so I went home.

September 8th – 2016

I got to Doug's around 7:00 because I needed to make a good trail to go in and out on in low light conditions. There were a lot of limbs that had fallen, nettles, raspberry bushes, and burdocks. Some places I needed a chain saw but didn't have one. We'll just have to be careful in those two places. I had brought some pink ribbon to hang up on the trail to help keep on the trail in the dark. I went down to the river and sat for two hours. I tried the slingshot thing again but couldn't stir anything up. It wouldn't throw a stone much more than twenty yards.

I went back in the afternoon and sat for about an hour when it started raining so I grabbed my bucket and was going to my truck but when I got in the woods I didn't even notice the rain. I decided to sit where Brian sits. I sat for another hour when the rain became a downpour. I grabbed my stuff and hurried to the truck which was 400 yards away. I got soaked but it was better than lying on your back in a brook.

September 9th – 2016

I went back to Montgomery and sat for two

hours and after seeing nothing I went and checked for tracks and once again there were none. Then I went back to Berkshire and sat for two more hours. After seeing nothing I started looking around for tracks and found none. I picked up and started for home but Doug was outside so I stopped and shot the breeze with him for a while. He asked if I had checked the corn up river. I said that I hadn't so I turned around and went back to check it out. I didn't go far before finding spots where they knocked down an acre spot at a time.

That afternoon I went back to Doug's and try a different spot. I didn't see anything and I left at dusk.

September 10th - 2016

I went into the corn next to the Benoit place in hopes of finding an easy access to the river. I learned quickly that this wasn't it. I went back to my truck and parked where I usually do and started checking the river out. There was a spot just down the river that you could walk across with a regular pair of rubber packs. So I went down and walked across to the island. From the island you could walk up the river another 300-400 yards.

I told Brian about this spot but he didn't act very interested. That afternoon I went to the first spot on the trail and sat until dark without seeing a thing. The reason I went down there instead of the island was to give Brian that spot if he changed his mind. I don't understand what is wrong with Brian. Maybe it's me hanging around there that he doesn't like Maybe I'll find another spot.

September 11th – 2016

I didn't go hunting because it was raining hard and the

wind was blowing hard. It was real nasty out there.

In the afternoon I went up on the mountain to an old apple orchard. I found a lot of sign but it just didn't feel right being there so I left and went to my spot in Montgomery. I sat for one and a half hours and didn't see anything. I haven't seen a track here since the third day.

September 12th –

The temperature was 26 degrees this morning compared to the 70's until now. Went back to Montgomery one last time to check for tracks and didn't find any. Got to find a new place or go back to Doug's, after all Brian's not hunting it.

I didn't go out in the afternoon.

September 18th – 2016

I haven't been out since day 12 kind of losing interest in it. I made a new target so I can shoot my crossbow at night to empty it.

Brian called tonight and said that the corn was getting cut in Berkshire. He thought that it would be a good idea if I went there and sat for a while in the morning.

September 19th – 2016

    I went there a little later than I normally would and as I was putting my camo on I spot a coyote out in the field. I grabbed my gun and took a shot and he took off running. I looked for blood and hair but I think it was a clean miss. Then I headed toward the corner of the meadow where the trail begins. Just as I get there I look in the edge of the corn and there is a fawn coming into the meadow. He is coming right to me and then he stops about ten yards away. We just stared at each other for a while. Then I talked to it very softly and slowly reached out to it and he was gone in two seconds. I checked all the usual places for tracks and didn't see any. I went by the ditch and sat for three hours and left. On my way to the truck I checked for any sign of a hit on the coyote still negative.

I went to Burn's for some crazy reason to check for tracks. I found some old ones then I found a fresh one coming out of the corn and it is fairly large so I know where I am sitting tonight.

I got there at 5:00 and at 6:40 I see a bear coming to me from my left side. Because of the way I was sitting, I would have to shoot right handed. I pulled up but couldn't hold it steady. I jumped up to my right trying to stay out of the bears sight. Then I pull the gun up to shoot left handed. I rest my right elbow on my right knee and leaned a little to the left to see the bear. He was slowly turning to go into the woods. I got the crosshairs on his shoulder and squeezed the trigger. It took off like it hadn't been hit so I was thinking the worst. I could see the bamboo moving so I know he has gone a ways. I get out of my blind and go down on the sand bar and I couldn't find anything at first. Then I find a track then blood and a lot of blood. It brought me right to the bamboo. I had to get on my hands and knees and crawl in. I had gone about ten feet when I look up and he is probably five feet from me and it looks like he is sitting there looking at me. I quickly pull the hammer back on my rifle and give it a poke in the butt. He has expired so I let the hammer down on my gun grab the bear by the back leg and try to move it but I couldn't. I went to see Forest to call Brian for help.

    I got to Forest's house and he was just going to bed. He handed me the phone and disappeared. I called Brian not only for his help and his four wheeler too. He said he would be there as soon as he could get his gear together. Then Forest comes down dressed for dragging a bear so we went back. When we got back to the barn yard the owner's wife was out there and we told her I had just got a bear. She said she was going to the house because she didn't want to see it. Then I showed him where the bear was and he took my rope and hooked onto it and we managed to get the bear out of the bamboo. We got it flopped around so I could take the guts out. About the time I got that done Brian was there with his machine. He had two pieces of rope which he tied together and with mine we were still 75 yards short. Forest and I started pulling on the bear. It moved a little easier without the guts but we were working hard. Brian had some low water boots on so he didn't come down even after I told him if he took on big step he may have one foot in a half inch of water. Forest and I got it close enough to tie the ropes together. When he started pulling he could only get 5-10 feet at a time then he would back up and reattach the rope. After a dozen times of this we got the bear on top of the bank and we all found a spot to sit on the machine and we rode up to the trucks. We managed to get the big sow on to my truck. Then we went to the store to get it weighed in. The bear weighed 182 pounds Thankyou Lord.

September 20th – 2016

Went down to show Doug and Norma my bear. They wanted to hear all about it. We had a nice chat and they thought it was a nice bear. Now it's off to brother Dan's place. Jean and Dan told me it was a nice one. Now off to brother Gary's to show him. He said nice one and that it looked heavier than it was. Now to show my son but he was sleeping so I went to mom and dad's. I backed next to the back porch to be close to the water to wash the bear out. Then I brought it to Ron Paquette to cut it up. He gave me eighty dollars off to put toward my book. Thanks Ron.

September 21st – 2916

Got up and went looking for deer and turkeys because the seasons start the first of October. I saw a few turkeys but no deer.

September 22nd – 2016

The doe permits are going to be drawn today. I ran into Carolyn and she told me about a place to check in the morning. I didn't see anything today. I checked on the permits and Brian got one for zone B and I got one for zone C so we won't be hunting together in December.

September 23rd – 2016

I got up and checked the spot out that I was told about and it was all she said it would be. I saw six birds and two had ten inch beards, two had eight inch beards and two were jakes with five inch beards. These are plus or minus a little in length. Shot my bow with Brian and thought that I did quite well. I hit black 4 out of 5 shots. The fifth one took off must be a tremor. I told him about the turkeys I had seen and he seemed excited about it.

September 24th – 2016

I went up and watched the birds this morning, can't wait for the season to start.

Brian and I went up there late afternoon and watched the birds in the pasture. He thought that they were real nice ones. We also saw three deer.

September 25th – 2016

I put two blinds up on Bulger's. One in the apple orchard and the other one down where my shooting shack used to be.

September 26th – 2016

Shot my bow again and about every other shot went flying into the pasture. I have got to control my tremors better.

September 27th – 2016

I took a trip to Montgomery Center to spot turkeys. The land is all posted and nobody will give you permission to hunt so I went home.

We shot our bows again in the evening.

September 28th – 2016

Took a ride to Montgomery and saw a bunch of them on Longley's. I can't get permission to hunt there either. I kind of thought if they could be on the Archambault Farm then I would try for them. But there are people renting his place so I didn't ask for permission to hunt there. We shot again this afternoon and I guess we are ready. We took a couple of days off to relax (I had a honey do list a mile long and had only two days to get it done.)

Turkey Season Oct. 1-22

Deer Season Oct. 1-31

October 1st – 2016

I got to my spot below Ken's by the big orchard an hour before sunrise. I sat for 3 ½ hours and didn't see a thing.

In the afternoon I sat in Ken's shack from 2-7 and didn't see a thing.

October 2nd – 2016

I went to my blind on Bulger's to watch the meadow. I sat for three hours and then I put my camera out by the only apple tree on my side of the meadow. On the way home I saw about a dozen turkeys trying to cross the road. I drove by them and went back by them and parked by the sap shed. I got out and wanted to get closer but I couldn't get over or under the fence so I went into the back of the sap shed and waited for 45 minutes. I didn't see them come across the road. So I got in my truck head for home but the birds were still there only up by Brown's house. I went home.

That afternoon on my way back to ken's shack I saw a bunch of turkeys in Mark's barnyard. I didn't stop because the whole family was outside watching them. I sat for five hours and saw nothing.

October 3rd – 2016

I didn't get up early this morning so around seven I went to Mark's to find out where the birds hide at night. I didn't have any luck seeing any birds so I decide to go to the center. I should have known better because the land is all posted. I saw a flock of four all toms and in the next field were a dozen hens with little ones. I don't have permission to hunt in any of the fields in the Center. I turned around and began to head for home. I stopped at Mark's to see if he knew where the birds were coming out. He told me that a big tom was coming out about every evening when they fed the cows in the pasture above the house. I decided to go into the woods to try to find him. I tried some calling but I didn't get any response then I left.

This afternoon I went back up on the hill but didn't sit in my blind. I sat closer to the apple tree on my side of field. After four hours of seeing nothing I left for home.

October 4th – 2016

I didn't go out in the morning because of a doctor's appointment. I found out that I need a partial knee replacement.

When I got back I went looking for turkeys but I didn't see any so I went up on the hill to change cards in my camera then sat in my blind I put in the apple orchard. I saw a lot of cars go by and zero deer. When I got home I checked the card and I had two pictures of me, four of a nice fat doe and one of a big black bear pulling on the limbs of the apple tree. I can't wait to sit there in the morning.

October 5th – 2016

In the morning had to bring my mother-in-law to the airport.

I left the house about three to go up to Hillwest and sit in my blind from 3:30 – 7:00. I didn't see anything. It is very disappointing.

October 6th – 2016

I planned on getting up early but slept until seven. I do get going around nine looking for turkeys. I didn't see any in the usual places. I stopped at Blair's sugar house and went in the little woods with a lot of apple trees looking for a good place to ambush a deer. I found several spots and I narrowed it down to one. If a person could spend a little time and effort they could have a nice spot there.

Then I went to change cards in my camera and then proceeded toward home but when I got to the Cabana farm I saw Mark's helper. I pulled into the yard and asked him about the turkeys. He told me that yesterday afternoon there was a flock by the water station and the big tom was with them. I thanked him and went home. In the afternoon I was going to hunt Hillwest in my blind by the field. I had to go right past the water station on my way up there and the birds were in the meadow. They were in the right corner of the meadow and the big tom was with them. I checked the layout of the land. There was a brush line between them and myself and in the bottom of the field was an opening where they got from one field to the other. I cranked up the string on my crossbow, put an arrow on it and then I started my stalk. I got to where I wanted to be. I tried calling but had to put my bow on the ground because it took both hands to operate my box call. Well they came a running so I had to pick up my bow and get it ready. I don't know if they saw me but they stopped on the other side of the brush. I had a hard time to tell which bird was which through the brush. After a few minutes of staring at each other my bow was getting heavy and I thought that I would scare them if I put it down. I could see one nice hen and there wasn't as much brush between us so I got her in my scope and squeezed the trigger. Nothing happened. I forgot the other safety so I push the other safety and took the shot. Feathers were flying everywhere and the hen started to hobble off. The other birds went back to the corner except for the tom. He went half way and stopped then he went to his hen. While he was doing his thing I set my bow down and called again. He came running right to me and stayed in the open. I had to pick my bow up and get him in my sights, which I did. The only thing I didn't do was cock the bow. I tried getting it cocked and when I looked back up they were all gone and I didn't know where they went in. I spent an hour and a half looking for the hen but didn't find her or any sign of her.

When I got home I made some phone calls to get a metal detector. My old buddy Dave had one that worked good after I fixed a broken wire in the battery compartment.

October 7th – 2016

I went back to the meadow and found my arrow in ten minutes. I decided to go to Lee's to check for birds. There was a flock of hens with their little ones at the feed cart next to the woods. I went through the woods until I came to an opening so I sat down and waited hoping that the birds will come my way when they get done eating. It wasn't long before I see them coming. The young ones first then the big hens. One steps into my crosshairs and I release my arrow. I shot just over the top of her. Now I walk back to the truck and get the metal detector and find my arrow in just a few minutes.

In the evening I went to Blair Farms and sat in the place that I picked out on my previous scouting of the area. I had been sitting for at least half an hour when I looked behind me and spot a hunter trying to sneak up on me. I waived to him to let him know that I was there and not a deer. He came up to me and apologized. He thought that I was a turkey. He went about seventy yards from me and sat down. He sat for maybe an hour and then he leaves by walking in the middle of the meadow. I sat until dark but didn't see anything.

October 8th – 2016

I went to Black Falls and went in where I did yesterday. I went to the same spot and sat for a while. After half an hour of sitting quiet I tried a call. I didn't get anything to respond so I stood up to leave and there they are coming my way. They saw me move and ran off. I decided to head for home and when I got to Frank's farm there were some birds in his cow yard. Some were young ones and there were some nice hens also but with the ground being cement I wouldn't dare to shoot my bow there. I hadn't asked him for permission to hunt here anyhow. I went home to wait for my evening hunt.

I went to Ken's shack and sat for four hours and I saw nothing and a lot of it.

October 9th – 2016

I was heading for Black Falls after getting up late but got side tracked when I came around a sharp corner by Lumbra's. The road was full of turkeys and I only hit one of them. I looked behind me and saw the hen hobbling away. It looked like it had two broken legs. I parked at Alfred's and walked up the road to the spot I saw the turkey last. I walked around the sharp corner and didn't see it. I went into the woods and walked back to Bunk's driveway and didn't see it. I walked down the drive to let Brian know that I was looking for a turkey. Then I went back into the woods again and went toward the sharp curve and could not find the bird. I did the same on the other side of the road and didn't see it so I left.

    I went to Black Falls and couldn't locate any birds so I went to Hillwest to check my camera. I changed cards and sat there for a while. I left to take a ride to get a bite to eat. After a small lunch I went back on the hill. I sat until dark and didn't see a thing. When I got home I checked my card to see what I had for ten second videos. It had 73 videos of which two were of a bear and the rest were of a doe and her fawn. I decided to sit there that afternoon. I didn't see anything probably because the apples were gone.

October 10th- 2016

Monday morning I had to finish carpet squares before I could go hunting. I started at 4 am and finished at 1:30 pm. Later I went for a ride instead of sitting somewhere because of my Lions club meeting. I saw some birds on the Cabana farm. I drove up behind the barn and parked. The birds were in front of the cement water tank so I snuck around to the back side and started crawling. When I got close to the end of the tank I picked my head up and was looking eye to eye with the dominate hen. She started cackling to warn her brood of danger but she never moved. I could have shot her but I thought there were some horses in the pasture but I didn't see them so I passed on her.

October 11th – 2016

I got up early but was moving slowly because of my truck being covered with frost. I didn't get to Cabana's until 7:30 and noticed the horses were in a different pasture. Better to be safe than sorry. I went on the Longley Bridge Road and spotted flock of turkeys. They were behind and beside the trailer across from Stan's. I passed on these turkeys because of their location.

Then I went on The Black Falls road and saw turkeys in the spot that I was going to sit at. I picked another spot and when I got there the cows saw me and wouldn't leave alone. I finally worked my way through the woods to the turkeys and I sat down and waited for them to finish eating. When they got filled up they went across the meadow instead of coming into the woods as usual. I tried getting in front of them but they saw me and ran into the woods.

I stopped and talked to Lee and he suggested that I set up by his house and shoot them on his lawn. As if that would happen.

October 12th – 2016

I got to Lee's before daylight and set up beside the barn and manure pile. I sat until noon and decided to go home to get a bite of something. Larry came to visit. We talked for an hour and then I suggested going for a ride to locate some turkeys. We went to an entirely different area and spotted a flock of 20 birds. I tried sneaking up on them but there were too many eyes to be successful. Before we knew it I had to go home and get ready to sit for the evening. I told him he could sit in Ken's shack but he had other plans. I went down and sat where my camera was. I thought I could hear something walking most of the evening but didn't see anything. I left when it go to dark to shoot.

October 13th – 2016

I went to Lee's on Black Falls about 6:30 am and was met by his dog. I didn't see any turkeys behind the barn. So I went to plan two but the turkeys were already moving. I thought that I could walk in the tall grass and find a place to ambush them but they saw me and ran off. I went and sat on a big rock hoping they would come back to me. I had to be home at 9:30 and when I stood up to leave the birds were coming right at me. They turned and ran away. Maybe another day. I took a ride in the afternoon and I got very tired. I actually fell asleep 3 times between the cold spring and Gerald's trailer. When I got to Bulger's I pulled over and parked and fell asleep in seconds. I had been there around half an hour when I heard a four wheeler go by then it comes back so I roll my window to see what the person wanted. "Mr. Jewett what are you doing up here?" he asked " You do know that you are not welcome up here anymore?" I was still groggy from my nap so I didn't respond right away. I knew who he was but couldn't put a name on that ugly face. Then he said "I know who you are and where you live so you hadn't better do anything wrong. I know that you are a deer jacker and I'm the one who got Mireka to have you move your shack. You don't think you're going hunting in there do you?" I told him that was exactly where I was going and that he should try to stop me. There isn't any posters on it and that there weren't any legal posters on the hill so I can hunt anywhere on the hill that I want until the owner tells me not to hunt on their land. He tells me not to hunt his land and that he was keeping an eye on me so don't stretch the rules. All I could say is whatever what a stupid reply. I should have gotten out of my truck put my work gloves on and knocked the crap out of that ugly s.o.b. I went down to my blind and didn't see a thing. I left early because someone was running up and down the road all evening. I'm sure it was my knew friend. I have to remain calm after all what can I do in the shape that I'm in.

October 14th – 2016

There was a pretty hard frost this morning. I got to Lee's before daylight but couldn't decide on a place to park my butt. The birds were coming and I was very uncomfortable and tried to hold still but my legs were aching and I just had to move them a little and they were gone. I left at 8:30 to go to my sons to work on his new project. I saw three deer and a flock of turkeys on my way to his house. This afternoon I went to Ken's shack and saw nothing and left when it got dark.

October 15th – 2016

This is the coldest morning yet. I found a place to sit right off I had the perfect cover for a shot. As it turned out there was a stump in the way of my limbs so I wouldn't be able to get a shot. The birds came out but not to me, then the beef came out and scared the birds away so I left to go to my sons. I got home about 1:00 and relaxed a couple of hours before going to Bulger's until dark and didn't see a thing.

October16th – 2016

I didn't go out this morning because I'm getting pretty sick of it I went to church instead. I went to Ken's shack for my evening hunt. It is nice and warm though it had rained earlier and is cloudy. It was around 6:20 when I see a deer coming into the orchard. I didn't have any windows open, so I try to open the front one. It squeeked and the deer is on alert. Then a doe and fawn come in from the right but it's too dark to see them through my sights and there is 10 minutes of shooting time left. The first one comes in and feeds right in front of me .It looked too small, we all know that there isn't a deer too small for Randy Jewett. Then I look down in the corner and there's a huge deer coming into the orchard. I try getting it in my scope but everything is black so I pack up and leave after changing cards in my camera. I had a lot of pictures of the little deer and none of the big deer.

October 17th – 2016

I went to Lee's and sat where I shot my bird in the spring. The turkeys didn't get the memo. After an hour of sitting I got up and went around the corner to check the manure pile. The birds saw me coming and flew away so I decided to look for the other flock that runs around on Lee's. I found them on a big rockpile. I couldn't see a way to sneak up on them so I went home. In the afternoon I went to Hillwest and sat in the blind close to the road. I saw a porcupine eating apples in a tree. That was all I saw.

October 19th – 2016

    Got up and went to Lee's early with a fool proof plan to get a turkey. My big plan was to lie on the manure pile until the birds came to feed. I guess it would have worked but my arm fell asleep and I couldn't raise my crossbow. I tried really hard to move my arm but it just didn't work. I couldn't even push the safety. I guess three hours is too long to sit or lay in one position. All I could do was watch until they see you and run away. I looked for the other birds but didn't find them. I left to go meet Arkie Pond to take down the old welcome to Richford signs but on the way over I spot 6 nice turkeys in a meadow and they were heading for the woods. I come up with a game plan. I turned around and park out of sight and go into the woods and try to get to the edge of woods before they do. I get within 15 yards from them. But they saw me and started walking away. I pulled the bow to my shoulder and looked through the scope and all I could see was black. I kept moving my head around to find a clear spot but they got away. I went through the woods after them again and got in front of them again. They saw me but kept coming angling away. A bird with a beard that was at least 10 inches long came within 20 yards of me I managed to find a clear spot in my scope and for a second could see the bird and I pulled the trigger. The feathers were flying all over. He started flying but landed after going maybe 25 yards. He started running. I didn't see him again after searching an hour. I caught up with Arkie and we finished our project. I went to Ken's shack this evening and didn't see anything.

October 20th – 2016

I went back to Lee's and couldn't find a bird. On the way off Black Falls I spotted a bunch of turkeys on Soule's land. They were in the road and I almost hit one of them. I couldn't find a place to park and shoot so I let them be.

Late morning and early afternoon Brian and I went to check out apple trees on Doug's. We found a lot of sign. It was raining hard in the evening so I sat in my truck watching the meadow Doug's. I didn't see anything.

October 21st – 2016

   Went for a ride on the Marvin Road looking for turkeys and found one flock. They were in Mark's back meadow by the small corn piece. I counted 20 + birds but left them alone because I had to help my son. It was raining again the afternoon so I sat at Doug's again and saw nothing again.

October 22nd – 2016

It was raining this morning so I went to my sons to work. I the afternoon I sat at Lee's from 5:00 -7:00 and didn't see a thing.

October 23rd – 2016

This is the last day of turkey hunting in zone c. I went to Lee's and checked out his pastures and saw nothing so I went for a short walk in the woods and found nothing. I went to Soule's and found nothing. I went to Burn's and there was a flock of twenty or more birds.

I parked by the covered bridge and went down to the edge of the river until I thought I was close to the birds. To get to the corn piece that they were in I had to go through a bunch of bamboo, brush and blow downs. Almost impossible to be quiet. When I got to where I could see the cornfield the birds were coming right to me. They were almost in range when they went out into the field out of range and when they got by me they came back to the edge of the woods then stopped in the corner.

    So I went into the woods and made my way to the corner. I looked in the corner and the birds were gone and Brian was standing by the bridge. I asked him if he had seen the turkeys and he had not. I went to Ken's shack tonight and saw that the apples are gone and the deer are gone too.

October 23rd – 2016

I went to zone b looking for turkeys but didn't have any luck. I went to Ken's shack in the afternoon and didn't have any luck.

October 24th - 2016

Went to Berkshire for turkeys and found a small flock but they were across the river from the pullout. I tried calling but couldn't get them to come across the river.

In the afternoon I sat below Ken's under a hemlock on a ledge and didn't see a thing.

October 25th –

I went back on the Marvin Road and the turkeys were on my side of the river. They were on top of Mark's meadow. I went back up the road just past the stone house and parked.

Years ago the dog lady built a wooden fence all the way around her property. A lot of it has fallen down. I climbed onto a piece of it and inti to planted spruce which is about 16 feet high and very thick.

There are some small openings with raspberry bushes in them. There are meadows above, to the right and to the left. On the one to the right, there is about 50 yards of woods with a small brook running through it.

    The meadow on the left has about a 100 yards of woods with a small apple orchard and small brook. It seems like a deer haven. The turkeys saw me and took off. I had a meeting that evening so I didn't go back today.

October 26th – 2016

Went to Mark's field on the Marvin Road and set up my decoys. I heard a crow caw and then a gobble. Hearing the gobble made me think I was close to being in the right place.

Shortly after sunrise I see the birds coming out and land to my right, another bunch landed to my left and a few landed right in front of me to check out my decoy. There were 2 jakes and 2 hens. I picked out the biggest jake pull my gun to my shoulder and got busted. Turkeys were running and flying everywhere. I still had a chance at the jake and squeezed the trigger but he flew away. All the other birds flew across the river but the jake landed in a tree on an island in the middle of the river. I slowly walked toward him and he flew away. Still have time to find more birds.

    I drove down the road about 2 miles and saw some more birds in Garrow's corn piece. There is an island in the middle of this corn piece. It consisted ledge, rocks, trees and old machinery. The birds were on the left side of it so I go to the right and try to get to the top before they do. When I got to the top the birds were above me in the field about 50 yards away. I can't hit a bird at 18 yards but I had to give it a try picked out the closest bird and took the shot. It jumped into the air landed and started eating again. I tried calling but they just ignored me. They worked their way into the woods so I left.

I met Brian about 10:00 am and we decided to take a ride to look for turkeys. It didn't take long for us to see a flock crossing the road.

We caught up with a few of them about 25 yards away all bunched together under a small spruce. I was waiting for him to shoot but he didn't. He wanted something bigger. We followed them for awhile but lost them. So it's back to the truck.

In the afternoon we went looking for turkeys for the next mornings hunt. We must have seen 200 birds, all within a mile of each other. Then we went back in the evening to put them to bed and couldn't find a bird.

October 27th – 2016

I set up on the Marvin Road again. Today I didn't hear or see anything so after sitting for an hour and a half I left.

I went looking where we saw all the turkeys yesterday But didn't find any. Then I went to Brian's barn but he wasn't there.

I decided to go across the road into the little patch of woods. I have been wanting to check this place out because it had a lot of apple trees that were loaded with apples. As I approached the guardrail I could see a deer feeding on the apples. After further observation I spotted another one. Brian went by while I was watching the deer. I went back to the barn and told him about the deer.

  I grabbed my bow and walked past the deer and went into the woods and after checking things out I decided that this was a good place for deer. It had lots of apples, a nice mixture of softwood and hardwood trees, 3 meadows within a hundred yards of it and water running through it. We later found out that this spot was off limits.

October 28th -2016

I set up on the Marvin Road again and didn't see anything. I went looking for Brian and found him at the barn. He saw just as much as I did. We decided to take a ride. We saw some birds but they were too far away for us to go after.

I went to Ken's in the afternoon and didn't see a thing.

October 29th – 2016

I set up 2 decoys on the Marvin road and sat until 7:30 I left early and walked around the field. I was almost to the pull off when I heard a hen cackle from the woods to my right. I jumped in the ditch and got ready to see some turkeys. They came flying from the trees and flew across the river. There were around 30 birds. I was getting sick of this game because they didn't play fair.

I went looking for Brian and found him at the barn. He had a little luck but it was bad. He had gotten on to some birds and shot and missed.

October 30th – 2016

I didn't get up until 6:15 on the last day of turkey hunting. It doesn't get light out until 7:00 so I still could make it. When I got to the Marvin Road I still had time to set up but decided to sit by my truck in case they fly down like before. I sat there until 8:30 and went looking for Brian to exchange boring stories. He didn't have anything to tell me then we went home.

    I called him around 1:00 to see if he wanted to try and locate some birds. He told me he was running an errand about an hour ago and saw some in Garrow's corn field. I picked him up and we went to check it out. When we got there we saw two deer but when we stopped to look at them they ran away. We went up uncle Dayton's road and out through the nation. We decide to go to Doug's and check some spots there. We didn't see any deer sign so we went back to go to the barn. When we got to Garrows' field there were birds where he had seen them earlier. While standing there trying to decide what to do. I look in the field and there's a turkey about thirty yards from us feeding. Then we slowly head back to the truck to get our guns. There were at least two birds going to the left side of the island, we went to the right side. Now the race is on to see who can get to the top first. The birds beat us and were going toward the woods. They are lucky that we are old and slow. Now to check the turkeys that are in the new meadow beside the corn field. They were heading into the woods about 150 yards away. I told him that I think those birds were coming to the corn field to cross the road and that we should go up to the edge of the woods and wait for them. He didn't think we would see them again. As we were standing there arguing the birds came into the field right where I said we should be. They were coming to the road but turned when they saw us. Now they were on top of the island heading to the left side. We went to the left side and then into the brush to ambush them when or if they came around. They were coming right to us but the position I was in I couldn't shoot and Brian was a couple feet in front of me. One bird came in close to him and he took a shot. The bird just shook his feathers and ran to the woods. The season ends and we had a lot of fun during bow and then shotgun seasons. We had so many chances and close calls that I never want to stop hunting these big birds.

November Rifle season

Day one

Got up at 4:15 I was so excited about the upcoming year because of all the deer we've seen. The feeling ended rather quickly because I don't hunt where we saw the deer.

When I got to the spot That I was going to sit at there was 20 minutes until shooting time. I sat for 3.5 hours and didn't see or hear a thing. I left and went to the store in Montgomery to see if any deer had been reported in. They had seven already.

I went up on Hillwest and sat in my blind on Bulger's. I watch a little patch of woods that leads to an uncut meadow. I sat there for 3 hours and didn't see a thing. I went home for a bite to eat. Now it is back to the woods for 2 more hours of sitting in my blind just to see nothing. Brian got a nice 4 pointer that weighed 148#. He made a good shot on it but couldn't find right off so he made some calls and got some help they found it in about 10 minutes. It had gone 75 yards.

Day -2

I got up the same time as yesterday and sat where I sat the first day. I sat for 3 hours then I took a little walk to check for sign. I wasn't impressed with what I saw. Then I went to my blind on Hillwest for three hours. I could hear something walking in the woods. It turned out to be a man in a red and black plaid coat with a camo hat and he was carrying a walking stick. He started walking through the middle the old meadow (something I wanted to do but was too lazy to do it). I got ready just in case he jumped up a deer. He only went as far as the old barn and started taking pictures. I decided to go home and get something to eat. In the afternoon I went to Ken's shack for 2.5 hours. I didn't see anything come out getting very disappointed.

Day-3

Got up again at 4:15and went on Westhill again. When I got down to the orchard I realized that I had forgotten my bucket to sit on. I looked around and found a rock to kneel beside and lean against.

    About half an hour later I heard something walking in the leaves behind me. Then I heard something to my right. My legs were aching so I stood up, looked at my watch. There were 3 minutes left until I could shoot. I looked up and saw a tail twitching and then I could make out the outline of a deer. I pulled the rifle to my shoulder but couldn't see the deer through my scope. I looked over the scope and I could see the deer so I tried looking through my scope again and I still didn't see the deer. It must have realized something was wrong and ran off. I sat another3 hours then went for a little walk but the leaves were really noisy so I left.

    That night I went to Berkshire to sit in Doug's shack I had to park on the main road and walk in. When I got to the road that goes to the shack I could see that someone was already in it. I decided to sit in the planted pines. I was glad that I had brought my bucket. I sat until it got dark and left I walked slowly hoping to see who was in the shack. He either went in a different direction or he stayed to make sure I was gone before he came out. I didn't go back the rest of the year.

Day - 4

I went back to the orchard and sat for 3.5 hours and went for a stroll looking for deer sign. I didn't see any deer or sign. I went home for a bite and to rest for a couple of hours.

I went back to Ken's shack and sat for four hours and didn't see anything. Thanks to my I Pad for keeping me company.

Day -5

I went to South Richford on the Grierson Road and sat in the apple trees. After three hours I went for a walk to check the place out. I had never deer hunted this area so I wandered around to learn the area. I didn't see anything so after 1.5 hours I went home for lunch and to rest.

I went back there in the afternoon for 4 hours and didn't see anything but a flock of turkeys. Some nice Toms in this group.

I didn't do much more hunting during rifle season because of my P. D. and I had a knee replacement the first week of November. I didn't get or even see a deer the rest of the season.

Muzzleloader Season

I didn't have any luck until the last afternoon. There was about 5 minutes of shooting time and I spot a 4 pointer or a buck with one horn that was forked. I had found a shed with a fork and I figured that they went together. I get a good broadside shot at him. He took off running on three legs. Like a fool I don't take my gun when I go after him. But it would have been after hours by the time I came on to him. But I could have probably got him. Any how I found him lying down but he jumped up and went over the bank going to the brook. I thought that Monday I would be able to find him by following his track and blood trail. I didn't know that we were going to get two feet of snow. I went to the last place that I had seen him. I couldn't tell where he went but I tried kicking the snow up hoping to find blood. I didn't find any so I made a lot of circles trying to find him but I didn't. I probably should have spent more time but it was hard going through the snow on a side hill.

THE END

2018 all seasons

This will probably be my last book so I'll tell you about my 2017 season. In the spring I got a turkey. It was a jake that weighed 16 lb. with a 5 inch beard. Due to the abundance of berries, apples, and nuts the bear were hard to find.

The regular deer season was about the same because of the amount of food in the woods.

I was given permission to hunt on the posted land between the pine cone and East Berkshire. The first morning I was on my bucket on a road between two meadows. It had been light for a while when I noticed two deer about 300 yards away and they were fighting. They suddenly stopped and then started chasing doe. The doe kept making circles and seemed to be coming my way. They disappeared in a ravine and I didn't see them for 20 minutes. Then I noticed a couple of deer in a corn field about 200 yards away and the went into the ravine that could bring the right to me. About ten minutes later they come out of the ravine coming straight at me. The first two were doe. The third was a six point buck being followed by a doe and an eight point buck. I thought that they were going full speed but when they saw me they found more gears. I tried a broadside shot at the eight pointer and missed. I should have waited for him to be going straight away, maybe next time.

I saw deer almost every morning but always in a different place. I did see 10 deer together on another day but didn't see any horns.

Thursday during muzzleloader season it was late afternoon with 10 minutes of shooting time left. I spot a buck coming up the trail and I'm waiting for a good shot. The deer turns and starts going away from me. I try putting the barrel of my gun out of the window and hit the side of the casing which makes a loud noise. The buck hears this and he turns and comes right to me. He stops about 30 yards away and I take aim on his neck and squeeze the trigger. When the smoke cleared I couldn't see the deer and was thinking I must have missed him. I go to the spot where I thought he was standing and can't find him. I start looking around and find him dead about ten yards away. I try to gut him out but I was shaking so hard I was afraid that I would get cut so

I stopped. Then I tried dragging him but didn't get very far. I left him there and went for help. I went to get Paul Sylvester Jr. He came and gutted the deer and dragged it to a spot where I could back up to the deer and he pulled it into the back of my truck and I didn't have to help him. I thanked him and he left. I went to Richford to weigh him at Pop a Top but they had closed early. I went to Brian's house and he went with me to Montgomery to weigh my deer and report it. It weighed 164# and had 8 points. I brought it back to Pop a Top to be weigh for the pool. They were closed but one of his men was there waiting for a truck to pick up his bottles and cans. He said he could do it and he brought the scale out and hooked up the deer to it. When he raised the deer, the strap slipped and the deer was still hitting my weights in the back of my truck and the deer weighed 119 #. He let it back down and slid the strap back up on the deer's leg and tried lifting it again and the same thing happened and he got a weight of 144 # so he let it down and asked me what they had for weight in Montgomery. I told him and that's what he wrote down on the pool which was the largest one. I noticed some people watching when we tried to weigh my deer and one was a relative of the guy that had a buck that weighed 150 give or take. He must have told the owner because the next time I went in it was listed at 144 #. I didn't want any trouble so I let it go. The guy probably needs the money more than I do.

About the Author

   I am 64 years old and suffer with PD. This will probably be my last book unless I write someone else's story. I wrote about my hunts in 2017 because there wasn't a lot to write about and if this is my last book I thought you my like to know. I am slowing down more each year but as long as I get excited about hunting I will try to get out there and enjoy myself.

   I had an operation on my brain called DBS deep brain stimulation. It has helped but I had hoped for more.

Dedication

I would like to dedicate this book to several people , Brian Jewett my hunting partner and best friend, also Paul Sylvester JR for helping me get my deer out of the woods.

I also would like to thank the farmers and land owners for giving me permission to hunt on their property. Doug King, Mark Brouillette, Mark St. Pierre, Lee Farrar, Jesse Soule, Alfred Gendron, Mr. Grierson, Stewart Archambault, Rich Burns, Hannas and Frank Adams.

PD

At times life with PD seems so hard,

But I have to grin and bear it.

I hope God plays the right card,

So a cure for this disease I get.

Sometimes I really get down,

Thinking about what I'm missing.

But life keeps going around,

So I should be counting my blessings.

I know that there is no cure

I just have to live with this thing.

Because I'll always have it for sure.

Now I wait to see what life will bring.

Someday it will get me,

And there will be more pain that's no lie.

Then really sick I will be,

And I'll probably die.

Randy A Jewett

Table of Contents

Spring Turkey Season --- 4

Bear Season-----------------26

Fall Bow Turkey,------------61
Deer Season

Nov. Rifle Season---------116

Muzzleloader Season---126

2018

DIARY OF A HUNTER BY RANDY A JEWETT

Made in the USA
Columbia, SC
10 April 2018